WOLFGANG AMADEUS MOZART

SERENADE a 6

for 6 Wind Instruments
für 6 Blasinstrumente
E♭ major/Es-Dur/Mi♭ majeur
K 375
Edited by/Herausgegeben von/Édition de
Harry Newstone

T0081228

Ernst Eulenburg Ltd

London · Mainz · Madrid · New York · Paris · Tokyo · Toronto · Zürich

CONTENTS

Performance material based on this edition is available from the publisher/
Der hier veröffentlichte Notentext ist auch als Aufführungsmaterial beim Verlag erhältlich/
Le matériel d'exécution réalisé à partir de cette édition est disponible auprès de l'éditeur
Eulenburg Chamber Series: ECS 1412–60

© 2008 Ernst Eulenburg & Co GmbH, Mainz
for Europe excluding the British Isles
Ernst Eulenburg Ltd, London
for all other countries

All rights reserved.
No part of this publication may be reproduced, stored in a retrieval system,
or transmitted in any form or by any means,
electronic, mechanical, photocopying, recording or otherwise,
without the prior written permission of the publisher:

Ernst Eulenburg Ltd
48 Great Marlborough Street
London W1F 2BB

PREFACE

On 3 November 1781 Mozart, in a letter to his father, Leopold, that included an account of how he spent his name-day (31 October), described the following interesting incident:

'At eleven o'clock at night I was treated to a serenade [Mozart uses the word *Nachtmusick*] performed by two clarinets, two horns and two bassoons – and that too of my own composition – for I wrote it for St Theresa's Day [15 October] for Frau von Hickel's sister, or rather the sister-in-law of Herr von Hickel, court painter, at whose house it was performed for the first time. The six gentlemen who executed it are poor beggars who, however, play quite well together, particularly the first clarinet and the two horns. But the chief reason why I composed it was in order to let Herr von Strack, who goes there every day, hear something of my composition; so I wrote it rather carefully. It has won great applause too and on St Theresa's Night it was performed in three different places; for as soon as they finished playing it in one place, they were taken off somewhere else and paid to play it. Well, these musicians asked that the street door might be opened and, placing themselves in the centre of the courtyard, surprised me, just as I was about to undress, in the most pleasant fashion imaginable with the first chord in E flat'. [1]

The work in question was what has come to be known as the Serenade in E flat, K 375 in its original sextet version, the combination of pairs of clarinets (or oboes, or sometimes English horns), horns and bassoons being more or less standard grouping for *Harmoniemusik* (Wind Band Music) at that time. That version is not too often heard these days having been superseded by the octet version (with two oboes added to the above combination) and one could wish that Mozart had left similar detailed documentation about the latter version's provenance.

On 23 January 1782 Mozart wrote to Leopold about 'young Prince Liechtenstein, who would like to collect a wind-instrument band (though he does not yet want it to be known), for which I should write the music.' [2] In April of that year the Emperor (Joseph II) established an official wind band of eight players to perform at court entertainments as well as on public occasions. [3] Wind ensembles so constituted were not entirely new in Vienna and elsewhere but the Emperor's example prompted other members of the aristocracy (the Princes Esterházy and Lobkowitz among them) to form similar groups for their musical establishments and, perhaps even more importantly, added further impetus for itinerant musicians to take their music into the streets, courtyards and public places of Vienna.

On 27 July 1782, Mozart wrote to his father: '[...] I have had to compose in a great hurry a serenade [Mozart here writes *Nacht Musique*], but only for wind instruments [...]' [4] He does not say for whom the work is being written but, with the Prince Liechtenstein's projected wind band (by

[1] *The Letters of Mozart And His Family*, transl. Emily Anderson (London, 1938), Vol. III, pp. 1155–56 (letter 431)

[2] op. cit., pp. 1183–84 (letter 442)

[3] *Neue Mozart-Ausgabe*, Series VII, Work Group 17, Vol. 2 (Kassel, 1979), Preface, p. VIII

[4] Anderson, op. cit., p. 1207 (letter 455)

now perhaps already in existence) as well as the Emperor's recently formed ensemble in mind, there seems to have been sufficient compulsion for Mozart to produce a work for wind octet and, since it had to be produced 'in a great hurry', it is not unreasonable to speculate that he would turn to the sextet written only nine months earlier and amplify it by the addition of a pair of oboes.

A comparison of the two autographs (now bound together in the Staatsbibliothek zu Berlin – Preußischer Kulturbesitz, Musikabteilung mit Mendelssohn-Archiv) shows, however, that this rearrangement was not simply a case of squeezing the two oboes into the existing texture. Mozart entirely rewrote the first, third and fifth movements, integrating the oboes so skilfully that it is impossible to tell that they are not part of the original conception, a process that necessitated extensive rewriting of the other parts and included some adjustments of phrasing, dynamics and sometimes notes, the more interesting of which are listed below in the Textual Notes. For the second and fourth movements (the two minuets) Mozart simply added the oboes on an empty stave above the horns in the autograph of the sextet version. Thus there are no minuets in the autograph of the octet score in Mozart's hand, but they are there (very neatly written) in another hand (COP8) which, in the opinion of Roger Hellyer, is that of Mozart's clarinettist friend, Anton Stadler.[5]

Editorial Notes

This present edition of the Serenade, K375 in its original version is based on the autograph score (AUT6). Where the autograph reading is not entirely clear reference has been made to the autograph score of the octet version (AUT8), but we have tried to differentiate between details that Mozart may have forgotten in writing out the later version and changes made as improvements or as second thoughts. The more important of these differences are listed in the Textual Notes below.

We abbreviate Mozart's *pia:* and *for:* to *p* and *f*. For those movements (III and IV) that begin quietly he wrote *p* or *pia:* but, with the exception of the first movement, the other movements have no starting dynamic, the standard practice for *forte* beginnings. These and other (or doubtful) dynamics, accidentals or staccatos are shown editorially in square brackets. Missing or possible slurs or ties are shown as broken ligatures and are usually based upon parallel or analogous passages; those which are not and are purely editorial suggestions, will be clear from the context and are identified as such in the Textual Notes below. Where both solid and broken slurs/ties are used over the same group, solid shows the autograph and broken are editorial suggestions.

Mozart's mixture of staccato dots and strokes makes it difficult to determine whether some difference between them in performance is intended. Perhaps it should be borne in mind that the quickest way to write a staccato dot (especially with a quill pen) is a short stroke. Sometimes in Mozart's autograph it is short enough to

---

[5] *NMA*, op. cit., p. X, fn 18

[6] Roger Hellyer, preface to Mozart's Serenade, K 375 (sextet version) (London, 1979)

look like a dot, and sometimes long enough to look like a stroke, but rarely within a pattern that consistently suggests a difference between the two. Since dots and strokes mean different things to today's performers we show staccatos throughout our score as dots except where the musical context suggests that an accented staccato would be appropriate, which interpretation seems occasionally to be supported by the autograph.[7]

Apart from the quaver grace notes in movement V, bb26, 30, 115, 119 and 120

(Cl. 1) Mozart's notation for grace notes throughout the Serenade is ♪ or ♪ (which was also how he wrote separate semiquavers) shown in this edition as ♪, and ♪ which we show as ♪. In COP8 movement II b49 (Trio) the grace notes are written ♪ in Cl. 1 and ♪ (?) in Cl. 2; in movement IV b3 (Cl. 1, 2) and b24 (Cor. 1, 2) they are all written ♪. Whether a grace note should be played long or short will depend on its context and must be left to the performer. Some redundant accidentals have been omitted.

Harry Newstone

---

[7] For a fuller discussion of this subject see Frederick Neumann, 'Dots and strokes in Mozart', *Early Music*, August 1993, pp. 429–53; Clive Brown, 'Dots and strokes in late 18th- and 19th-century music', *Early Music*, November 1993, pp. 593–610; and *Die Bedeutung der Zeichen Keil, Strich und Punkt bei Mozart*, ed. Hans Albrecht (Kassel, 1957)

VORWORT

Am 3. November 1781 beschrieb Mozart in einem Brief an seinen Vater Leopold, in dem er unter anderem auch erzählt, wie er seinen Namenstag (31. Oktober) verbrachte, folgende interessante Begebenheit:

„[...] auf die Nacht um 11 uhr bekamm ich eine NachtMusick von 2 clarinetten, 2 Horn, und 2 Fagott – und zwar von meiner eigenen komposition. – diese Musick hatte ich auf den theresia tag [15. Oktober 1781] – für die schwester der fr: v: Hickl, oder schwägerin des H: v: Hickl |:Hofmaler:| gemacht; alwo sie auch wirklich das erstemal ist producirt worden. – die 6 Herrn die solche exequirn sind arme schlucker, die aber ganz Hüpsch zusammen blasen; besonders der erste clarinettist und die 2 Waldhornisten. – die haubtursache aber warum ich sie gemacht, war, um dem H: v: strack |:welcher täglich dahin kömmt:| etwas von mir hören zu lassen. und deswegen habe ich sie auch ein wenig vernünftig geschrieben. – sie hat auch allen beyfall erhalten. – Man hat sie in der theresia nacht an dreyerley örter gemacht. – denn wie sie wo damit fertig waren, so hat man sie wieder wo anders hingeführt und bezahlt. – die Herrn also haben sich die hausthüre öfnen lassen, und nachdemm sie sich mitten im Hof rangirt, mich, da ich mich eben entkleiden wollte, mit dem Ersten E B accord auf die angenehmste art von der Welt überrascht."[1]

Das betreffende Werk ist inzwischen als Es-Dur-Serenade, KV 375, in der Originalfassung für Sextett bekannt; die Kombination bestimmter Instrumentenpaare – je zwei Klarinetten (oder Oboen oder manchmal Englischhörner), Hörner und Fagotte – war damals mehr oder weniger die Standardbesetzung der „Harmoniemusik" genannten Bläserensembles. Die Originalfassung wird heute nicht so oft gespielt, meist wird die spätere Oktettfassung (mit der oben erwähnten Standardbesetzung und zwei Oboen) vorgezogen. Man wünschte sich nur, daß Mozart die Entstehungsgeschichte dieser späteren Fassung auch so detailliert beschrieben hätte.

Am 23. Januar 1782 schrieb Mozart an Leopold: „[...] der Junge fürst liechtenstein, |:er will es aber noch nicht wissen lassen:| dieser will eine Harmonie Musick aufnehmen, zu welcher ich die stücke setzen soll"[2]. Im April desselben Jahres gründete der Kaiser (Joseph II) ein offizielles Bläserensemble, dessen acht Musiker sowohl bei Hof zur Unterhaltung als auch bei öffentlichen Anlässen aufzuspielen hatten.[3] Solcherart bestallte Bläsergruppen waren weder in Wien noch anderswo ganz neu, aber das Beispiel des Kaisers veranlaßte andere Mitglieder der Aristokratie (u. a. die Fürsten Esterházy und Lobkowitz), ihren herrschaftlichen Hauskapellen ebenfalls solche Bläserensembles anzugliedern und gab – was wohl noch wichtiger war – herumziehenden Wandermusikern einen zusätzlichen Anstoß, ihre Musik auf den Straßen, Innenhöfen und öffentlichen Plätzen Wiens vorzutragen.

[1] vgl. *Mozart. Briefe und Aufzeichnungen*. Gesamtausgabe, hg. von der Internationalen Stiftung Mozarteum Salzburg, gesammelt (und erläutert) von Wilhelm A. Bauer und Otto Erich Deutsch, Kassel etc. 1962/63 [im folgenden Bauer-Deutsch], Bd. III, Nr. 638, S. 171–172

[2] ebda., Bd. III, Nr. 660, S. 194
[3] *Neue Mozart Ausgabe*, Reihe VII, Werkgruppe 17, Bd. 2, Kassel 1979, Vorwort, S. VIII

Am 27. Juli 1782 schrieb Mozart an seinen Vater: „[...] ich habe geschwind eine Nacht Musique machen müssen, aber nur auf harmonie"[4]. Zwar erwähnt er nicht, für wen das Werk gedacht war, aber im Hinblick auf Fürst Liechtensteins geplante (oder vielleicht bereits bestehende) Bläsergruppe und das neue Ensemble des Kaisers gab es für Mozart sicher zwingende Gründe ein Werk für Bläseroktett zu schreiben. Da das Werk „geschwind" gebraucht wurde, bietet sich die Vermutung an, daß Mozart das neun Monate vorher komponierte Sextett nahm und es um zwei Oboenstimmen erweiterte.

Ein Vergleich der beiden Autographe (in der Musikabteilung der Staatsbibliothek zu Berlin – Preußischer Kulturbesitz, in einem Band zusammengebunden) zeigt jedoch, daß die Oboen bei der Bearbeitung nicht einfach irgendwie in die bestehende Textur hineingezwängt wurden. Mozart hat die Sätze I, III und V völlig neu bearbeitet und dabei die Oboen so kunstvoll eingegliedert, daß man nie darauf käme, sie wären nicht Teil des ursprünglichen Entwurfes gewesen. Dieser Vorgang erforderte jedoch eine weitgehende Umschreibung der anderen Stimmen, zum Teil mit Änderungen in Artikulation, Dynamik und Notentext; die interessantesten werden nachstehend in den Einzelanmerkungen aufgeführt. In Satz II und IV fügte Mozart die Oboen einfach im Autograph der Sextettfassung in ein leeres System über den Hörnern ein. Die Menuette im Autograph der Oktettfassung sind deshalb nicht in Mozarts Hand, sondern wurden dort – sehr sauber – von einem Kopisten (COP8) eingetragen. Roger Hellyer meint, es sei die Hand von Mozarts Freund, dem Klarinettisten Anton Stadler.[5]

[4] Bauer-Deutsch, a.a.O., Bd. III, Nr. 680, S. 214
[5] *NMA*, a. a. O., S. X, Fußnote 18

Revisionsbericht

Die vorliegende Ausgabe der Serenade KV. 375 beruht in ihrer Originalfassung auf der autographen Partitur (AUT6). Wenn die autographe Lesart nicht eindeutig ist, wurde die Autographpartitur der Oktettfassung (AUT8) hinzugezogen; es wurde allerdings versucht zwischen den Details, die Mozart bei der Reinschrift der späteren Fassung vergessen haben mag und den Änderungen, die er als Verbesserungen ansah oder die ihm neu eingefallen waren, zu unterscheiden. Die bedeutenderen Unterschiede sind im Revisionsbericht erwähnt. Beide Autographe haben Querformat und sind auf Papier mit jeweils 12 Systemen notiert. Mozart schrieb weder Titel noch Datum auf die Partituren und signierte sie auch nicht. In der Hand von André, dem Verleger der Erstausgabe der Oktettfassung (Offenbach 1810), steht jedoch auf der Sextettpartitur „Wien im Monat Oktober 1781" und auf der Oktettpartitur „1782 in Wien".[6] Wir haben Mozarts Partituranordnung (von oben nach unten: Hörner, Oboen, Klarinetten, Fagotte) dem heutigen Gebrauch angepaßt.

Mozarts *pia:* und *for:* haben wir *p* und *f* abgekürzt. Bei den leise anfangenden Sätzen (III und IV) schrieb er *p* oder *pia:* vor; die anderen Sätze, mit Ausnahme von I, haben allerdings keine Dynamikvorschriften am Satzanfang, was in der zeitgenössischen Aufführungspraxis *forte* bedeutete. Diese und andere (oder zweifelhafte) Dynamikangaben, Akzidenzien oder Staccatoangaben sind durch eckige Klammern als vom Herausgeber stammend gekennzeichnet. Fehlende oder denkbare Halte- oder Bindebögen werden gestrichelt wiedergegeben und basieren normalerweise auf analogen Passagen oder Parallelstellen.

[6] Roger Hellyer (Hrsg.), Vorwort zu Mozarts Serenade KV 375 (Sextettfassung), London 1979

Andere, die lediglich Vorschläge des Herausgebers sind, ergeben sich aus dem Zusammenhang und sind in den Einzelanmerkungen ausgewiesen. Wo sowohl durchgezogene als auch gestrichelte Legato- oder Haltebögen über derselben Notengruppe verwendet werden, stammen durchgezogene Bögen aus dem Autograph und gestrichelte zeigen Herausgeberzusätze an.

Mozart verwendete eine Mischung aus Staccatopunkten und -strichen [Keilen], es ist schwer zu entscheiden, ob er damit verschiedene Ausführungen anzeigen wollte. Man sollte vielleicht in Betracht ziehen, daß sich ein Staccato (besonders mit einem Federkiel) am schnellsten als kurzer Strich schreiben läßt. In dieser Partitur sind diese Staccatostriche manchmal so kurz, daß sie wie Punkte aussehen und manchmal lang genug, um als Striche gelten zu können. Die Schreibweise hält sich aber selten an ein Muster, das auf einen konsequent durchgeführten Unterschied schließen ließe. Da Punkte und Striche heute eine andere Bedeutung haben, werden die Staccati durchweg als Punkte notiert, als Striche nur dann, wenn im musikalischen Zusammenhang ein betontes Staccato besser paßt; auch das Autograph scheint diese Auslegung an mehreren Stellen nahezulegen.[7]

Abgesehen von den Achtelvorschlägen in Satz V, Takt 26, 30, 115, 119 und 120 (Kl. 1) schrieb Mozart die Verzierungsnoten in dieser Serenade überall als ♪ oder ♪ (so wie er auch einzeln stehende Sechzehntel notierte), sie werden in dieser Ausgabe als ♪ gedruckt, ♪ wird als ♪ gezeigt. In COP8, Satz II, T. 49 (Trio) sind die Verzierungsnoten in Kl. 1 als ♪ notiert und in Kl. 2 als ♪ (?); in Satz IV, T. 3 (Kl. 1, 2) und T. 24 (Cor. 1, 2) sind sie alle als ♪ notiert. Die Interpretation solcher Vorschlagsnoten (d.h. kurz oder lang) hängt vom Zusammenhang ab und bleibt den Ausführenden überlassen. Überflüssige Akzidenzien wurden zum Teil kommentarlos weggelassen.

Harry Newstone
Übersetzung: Judith Meier

---

[7] Zur ausführlicheren Erörterung vgl. Frederick Neumann, „Dots and Strokes in Mozart", *Early Music*, August 1993, S. 429–53; Clive Brown, „Dots and strokes in late 18th- and 19th-century music", Early Music, November 1993, S. 539–610; außerdem *Die Bedeutung der Zeichen Keil, Strich und Punkt bei Mozart*, Hans Albrecht (Hrsg.), Kassel 1957.

PRÉFACE

Le 3 novembre 1781, retraçant dans une lettre à son père, Leopold, comment il avait passé le jour de sa fête (le 31 octobre), Mozart rapporta l'intéressante anecdote suivante:

« A onze heures du soir on m'offrit une sérénade (Mozart utilise le mot *Nacht-Musick*) jouée par deux clarinettes, deux cors et deux bassons – qui était également de ma composition, car je l'ai écrite pour le jour de la Sainte-Thérèse (15 octobre) à l'intention de la sœur de Frau von Hickel, ou plus exactement de la belle-sœur de Herr von Hickel, peintre de la cour, chez qui elle fut donnée pour la première fois. Les six gaillards qui l'exécutèrent étaient de pauvres mendiants qui, néanmoins, jouèrent très bien ensemble, en particulier la première clarinette et les deux cors. Cependant, la principale raison pour laquelle je l'ai composée était de faire entendre une pièce de ma composition à Herr von Strack qui passe en visite tous les jours. J'y ai donc mis beaucoup de soin. Elle fut également très applaudie et fut jouée dans trois endroits différents le soir de la Sainte-Thérèse, car dès que les musiciens avaient fini de la jouer quelque part, on les emmenait ailleurs et les payait pour la rejouer. En bref, ces musiciens se firent ouvrir la porte donnant sur la rue et, s'étant regroupés au mileu de la cour, me surprirent de la plus agréable façon qui se puisse imaginer, alors que j'aillais me dévêtir, par le premier accord de *mi* bémol. » [1]

L'œuvre en question allait devenir célèbre comme Sérénade en *mi* bémol, K.375, dans sa version originale pour sextuor à vent, regroupant deux clarinettes (hautbois ou parfois cors anglais), deux cors et deux bassons, selon la formation plus ou moins standardisée de l'*Harmoniemusik* (ensemble d'harmonie) de l'époque. Cette première version, peu donnée aujourd'hui, a été supplantée par la version pour octuor à vent (avec deux hautbois ajoutés à la précédente formation) sur l'origine de laquelle on aurait aimé que Mozart fût aussi prolixe.

Le 23 janvier 1782, Mozart écrivit à Leopold au sujet du «jeune prince Liechtenstein, qui aimerait rassembler un ensemble à vent (bien qu'il ne désire pas encore que cela se sache) pour lequel j'écrirais de la musique»[2]. En avril de la même année, l'empereur Joseph II fonda un ensemble à vent officiel de huit musiciens qui devait se produire lors des festivités de la cour et des célébrations publiques[3]. De tels ensembles d'instruments à vent n'étaient pas véritablement nouveaux à Vienne et ailleurs mais l'exemple de l'empereur incita d'autres membres de l'aristocratie (les princes Esterházy et Lobkowitz, entre autres) à doter leurs institutions musicales de formations similaires et – ce qui est sans doute plus important – encouragea les musiciens itinérants à se produire dans les rues, les cours et les places publiques de Vienne.

Le 27 juillet 1782, Mozart écrivit à son père: «J'ai dû composer en grande hâte une sérénade (Mozart emploie ici *Nacht*

[1] *The Letters of Mozart and His Family*, traduction anglaise d'Emily Anderson, London, 1938, vol. III, pp. 1155/56 (lettre 431)

[2] ibid., pp. 1183–84 (lettre 442)
[3] *Neue Mozart-Ausgabe*, série VII, vol. 17, Kassel, 1979, préface, p. VIII

Musique), mais pour instruments à vent sculs»[4]. Il ne précise pas à qui était destinée l'œuvre mais, connaissant le projet d'orchestre à vent du prince Liechtenstein (peut-être déjà constitué à ce moment-là) ainsi que l'existence du nouvel ensemble établi par l'empereur, les occasions offertes à Mozart de composer une œuvre pour octuor à vent ne manquaient pas. Comme celle-ci dut être écrite «en grande hâte», on peut raisonnablement imaginer que Mozart a repris le sextuor composé quelques neuf mois plus tôt et l'a augmenté par l'adjonction de deux hautbois.

La comparaison des deux manuscrits autographes (actuellement réunis sous la même reliure à la Staatsbibliothek zu Berlin – Preussischer Kulturbesitz, Musikabteilung) montre, toutefois, que cet arrangement n'a pas simplement consisté à incorporer les hautbois dans la trame existante. Mozart réécrivit entièrement les premier, troisième et cinquième mouvements en y intégrant les hautbois si adroitement qu'il est impossible de déceler qu'ils n'ont pas fait partie de la conception originale. Ce procédé nécessita la réécriture de longues séquences des autres parties et entraîna certaines modifications de phrasés, de nuances et parfois de notes dont les principales sont recensées dans l'appareil critique ci-dessous. Dans les deuxième et quatrième mouvements (les deux menuets), Mozart nota simplement les parties de hautbois sur une portée vide au-dessus des cors dans le manuscrit autographe de la version pour sextuor. Le manuscrit autographe de l'octuor ne comporte pas la transcription des menuets par Mozart, ceux-ci y apparaissent soigneusement copiés par un autre scripteur (cop8) qui serait, d'après Roger Hellyer, l'ami clarinettiste de Mozart, Anton Stadler[5].

---

[4] Emily Anderson, op. cit., p. 1207 (lettre 455)
[5] *NMA*, ibid., p. X, fn 18

Notes éditoriales

Cette édition dans sa version originale de la *Sérénade*, K.375, se fonde sur la partition autographe (source AUT6). Lorsque ce manuscrit autographe n'est pas assez clair, nous avons pris comme référence le manuscrit autographe de la version pour octuor (AUT8). Nous nous sommes toutefois efforcés de distinguer les détails que Mozart aurait pu omettre en transcrivant cette dernière version des changements qu'il aurait apportés pour améliorer sa partition ou des modifications qu'il aurait décidées ultérieurement. Les plus significatives de ces différences sont énumérées dans l'Appareil critique ci-dessous. Les deux autographes sont copiés sur du papier de format oblong (à l'italienne) réglé à 12 portées. Mozart n'a porté ni titre, ni date (ni même sa signature) sur aucune des deux partitions, cependant André, éditeur de la première édition de la version pour octuor (Offenbach 1810)[6], a noté les mots «Wien im Monat Oktober 1781» sur la partition du sextuor et «1782 in Wien» sur la partition de l'octuor. Nous avons changé l'ordre de disposition des instruments suivi par Mozart (de haut en bas: cors, clarinettes, bassons) pour nous conformer à l'usage actuel.

Les indications *pia:* et *for:* de Mozart ont été abrégées et remplacées par *p* et *f*. En tête des mouvements commençant doucement (III et IV), Mozart a indiqué *p* ou *pia:* mais, à l'exception du premier mouvement, les autres mouvements ne sont précédés d'aucune indication dynamique selon l'usage en vigueur qui impliquait ainsi de commencer dans la nuance *forte*. Celles-ci et d'autres indications dynamiques, altérations accidentelles ou staccatos manquants ou incertains ont été placés entre crochets à l'édition. Les liaisons et liaisons de phrasé absentes ou possibles ont été

---

[6] Roger Hellyer éd., Préface de la Sérénade, K.375, de Mozart (version pour sextuor), London, 1979

ajoutées sous forme de tracé discontinu et sont généralement reprises de passages parallèles ou analogues. Celles qui ne le sont pas et relèvent des suggestions éditoriales pures sont isolées du contexte et répertoriées comme telles dans l'appareil critique ci-dessous. Lorsqu'un même groupe est surmonté à la fois de liaisons continues et discontinues, la liaison continue se conforme au manuscrit autographe tandis que la liaison discontinue indique la suggestion des éditeurs.

Il est difficile de déterminer, du fait du mélange pratiqué par Mozart des points de staccato et des tirets, si leur interprétation doit être différenciée. Il faut sans doute garder présent à l'esprit que le moyen le plus rapide de noter un point de staccato (surtout à la plume d'oie) est de tracer un tiret court. Celui-ci, dans la partition, est parfois aussi court qu'un point ou aussi long qu'un tiret, mais adopte rarement une forme qui marque avec cohérence une distinction entre les deux. Les points et les tirets recouvrant deux notions distinctes pour les interprètes d'aujourd'hui, nous avons indiqué tous les staccatos de la partition par des points sauf quand le contexte musical appelle un staccato accentué, confirmé dans certains cas par le manuscrit autographe [7].

A l'exception des agréments en croches des mesures 26, 30, 115, 119 et 120 du mouvement V (Cl.1), la notation de Mozart dans toute la Sérénade des notes d'agrément est ♪ ou ♪ (qui est également sa façon de noter les doubles croches isolées) transcrite ♪ dans notre édition, et ♪ que nous avons transcrit ♪. Dans la source cop8, les agréments de la mesure 49 (Trio) du mouvement II sont notés ♪ à la Cl.1 et ♪ (?) à la Cl.2; ceux des mesures 3 (Cl.1., 2) et 24 (Cor.1, 2) du mouvement IV sont tous notés ♪. La durée brève ou longue de l'agrément dépend du contexte et doit être laissée au choix de l'interprète. Certaines altérations accidentelles redondantes ont été supprimées.

Harry Newstone
Traduction : Agnès Ausseur

---

[7] Pour un débat plus complet à ce sujet voir: Frederick Neumann, "Dots and strokes in Mozart" in *Early Music*, août 1993, pp. 429–453; Clive Brown, "Dots and strokes in late 18th- and 19th-century music" in *Early Music*, novembre 1993, pp. 593–610; et *Die Bedeutung der Zeichen Keil, Strich und Punkt bei Mozart*, éd. Hans Albrecht, Kassel, 1957

Textual Notes

AUT6 = Mozart's autograph MS of the Sextet version
AUT8 = Mozart's autograph MS of the Octet version
COP8 = Movements II, IV of the Octet, in another hand
      Both autographs located, and bound together, in: Staatsbibliothek zu Berlin-
      Stiftung Preußischer Kulturbesitz, Musikabteilung (*D-B* Mus. ms. autogr. W. A.
      Mozart 375)
b(b) = bar(s)   m = minim   sb = semibreve
n(n) = note(s)   cr = crotchet   q = quaver etc.

Mov. I

             Allegro maestoso from AUT8

bar	
5–6, 7–8,9–10	AUT8 dotted figure phrased 𝅗𝅥♪
6–7,8–9	(also bbl18–119, 120–121) Cl. 1 ♩*fp* 𝅗𝅥. as AUT8; AUT6 ♩*fp* 𝅗𝅥.
25,29	Cor. 1,2 nn3–5 stacc. by analogy with AUT8; ditto bbl37, 141 (see b113 below)
33–34	Fg. 2 AUT6 slur crosses barline
35	Cl. 1, 2 nn2–5 AUT8 Ob. 1, Cl. 1 no slur
38,39	Fg. 2 AUT6 one-bar slurs but two-bar slurs bb40–41, 42–43; AUT8 no slurs
66	Cor. 1 nn4–6 as AUT6
67	Cl. 1, b68 Cl. 2, b72 Fg. 1, b73 Fg. 2 nnl–8 slurs by analogy with AUT8 bb72, 73 Fg. 1, 2; similarly b74 Fg., 1, 2, b75 Cl. 1, 2, also parallel passages at bb189ff., 194ff. where slurs lacking in both versions
71	Cor. l, 2 *p* from AUT8
76–78	Cl. 1 AUT6 nn2–5 slur; slur across barlines by analogy with bb78–79 (AUT6); bb76–80 slurs across barlines in AUT8
76–79	Fg. 2 nn1–9 slurs by analogy with bbl98–201 Fg. 1
92	Repeats of bbl–92 (Exposition), bb93–216 (Development/Recapitulation) not in AUT8
101	After this bar AUT6 has empty bar crossed out
107	Cl. 1 *portato* phrasing from AUT8
108	Cl. 1 AUT6 nn1–4 slur, extended editorially to n5 as AUT8
108,109	Fg. 2 nl AUT6 B♮ , AUT8 C♭ (more logical)
112	AUT8 all parts ⟨
113–147	AUT6, AUT8 not written out, instead the instruction 'Da Capo 35 Täckt'
153, 157	Cor. 1 nn5–8 stacc. by analogy with Cl. 1 bbl61, 165
176	Cl. 1 nn2–8, Cl. 2 nn 1–9 slurs by analogy with AUT8
218	Cl. 2, Fg. 1, 2 AUT6 nl *sf* (perhaps written mechanically after b217) adjusted to *fp* as other parts and all parts in AUT8

XVI

219,221,

223   Cl. 1, 2, Cor. 1, 2 *fp* as AUT6, AUT8 (unlike bb3, 115 where both sources separate *f* and.*p* as we show)

229   Cor. 1, 2 AUT6 n2 g' in error, adjusted to e' as in AUT8

Mov. II

9   Fg. 1, 2 originally m as b11

21–28   AUT6 not written out, instead the instruction after b20 'Da Capo fino a 𝄐 ' the fermata being in b8; Fg. 2 (Fg. 1 not written out) b8 has a fermata above and below n1 indicating the end of the movement, i.e., nn2, 3 are not to be played. The present edition separates the *fine* bar for the convenience of performing material.

56   Fg. 1 AUT6 originally [music notation] altered (not slur?) to [music notation], the change possibly made for the Octet version where nn2–3 slur in COP8

Mov. III

6   Cl. 1 nn 1–2 slur by analogy with AUT8; cf. AUT6 b53

7   Cl. 1 nn 1–4 slur by analogy with b54

13,14   Fg. 1 AUT8 phrased | [music notation] |

23   Ob. 1 AUT8 phrased | [music notation]

26   Cl. 1, Fg. 1 AUT88 marked *dolce* from n2

30,31   Dynamics from AUT8

46   Cl. 2 phrasing by analogy with b82 Cl. 1

59   Cl. 2 nn4–5 slur by analogy with AUT8 Ob. 1 (nn6–7), added on this basis to Cor. 1 nn2–3

60   Cl. 2 nn2–3 slur by analogy with AUT8 Ob. 1

Mov. IV

14   Cl. 1 n3, b15 AUT6 originally octave lower

15   Fg. 2 AUT6 unclear, original possibly [music notation]

21   Cl 1, Fg. 2 AUT6 m followed by 2 cr rests (uncorrected)

41   Cl. 1, 2 nn2–3 (upbeat to b42) slur based on context, shown in no source

Mov. V

2,6   (also bb14, 59, 63, 71, 165, 169, 177) Cl. 2 AUT8 (Ob. 2, Cl. 2) [music notation]

4   Ob. 1 ᴀᴜᴛ8 clearly ♩♪♪♪♪♩♪ (Ob. 2 less clearly); Cl. 1, 2 not written out (marked 'Col 1mo oboe' and 'Col 2do oboe'); ditto b61 (not written out – at b59 the instruction'Dal segno 𝄋 ohne Repetition bis 𝅝 '

39   Cor. 1 nn3–4 slur by analogy with ᴀᴜᴛ8 Ob. 1

55   Fg. 1 ᴀᴜᴛ6 slur from nI to b58 n1, we adjust as Cl. 1

74ff.   (from upbeat) No dynamics in either version, *p* suggested here, or possibly at Cl. 1 upbeat to b110 (NB, *f* both versions b121)

83   Cl. 1, 2 slurs by analogy with ᴀᴜᴛ8

91   Cl. 1, b93 Cl. 2 n6 ᴀᴜᴛ8 (Cl. 1, Ob. 1 respectively) b♮

98,99   Fg. 1 suggested editorial accidentals (over stave) from ᴀᴜᴛ8 Cl. 2; similarly b100 Cl. 1 from ᴀᴜᴛ8 Ob. 1

129   Fg. 1, 2 *f* by analogy with ᴀᴜᴛ8

135   Cl. 1 n2, Cl. 2 n4 ♭ possible on basis of ᴀᴜᴛ8

164ff   From preceding upbeat, ᴀᴜᴛ6 not written out, instead the instruction 'Da Capo fino a 𝄐' but Mozart forgot to write the 𝄐; logically it would have been over the repeat sign in b16

209   Fg. 2 n2, b210 originally octave higher

Harry Newstone

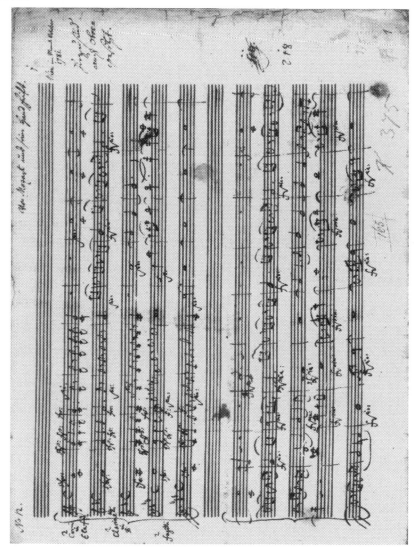

Mozart, Serenade a 8, K 375, Autograph MS
D-B Mus.ms.autogr. W. A. Mozart 375, p. 1
Staatsbibliothek zu Berlin – Preußischer Kulturbesitz,
Musikabteilung mit Mendelssohn-Archiv
Reproduced by permission © bpk

SERENADE a 6

Wolfgang Amadeus Mozart
(1756–1791)
K 375

I. [Allegro maestoso]

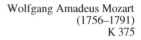

Edited by Harry Newstone
© 2008 Ernst Eulenburg Ltd
and Ernst Eulenburg & Co GmbH

2

4

6

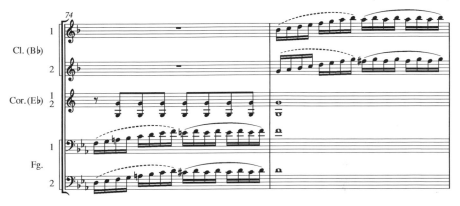

10

16

II. Menuetto

22

Menuetto da capo

24

III. Adagio

Clarinetto (B♭)

Corno (E♭)

Fagotto

Cl. (B♭)

Cor. (E♭)

Fg.

Cl. (B♭)

Cor. (E♭)

Fg.

26

28

IV. Menuetto

Trio

Menuetto da capo

V. Finale

Allegro

Clarinetto (B♭)

Corno (E♭)

Fagotto

Cl. (B♭)

Cor. (E♭)

Fg.

Cl. (B♭)

Cor. (E♭)

Fg.

42

44